EGYPT

Written by Rod Barkman

COUNTRIES of the WORLD

PowerKiDS press

Published in 2025
by The Rosen Publishing Group, Inc.
2544 Clinton Street, Buffalo, NY 14224

Written by: Rod Barkman
Edited by: Elise Carraway
Designed by: Amelia Harris

Cataloging-in-Publication Data

Names: Barkman, Rod.
Title: Egypt / Rod Barkman.
Description: Buffalo, NY : PowerKids Press, 2025. | Series: Countries of the world | Includes glossary and index.
Identifiers: ISBN 9781499447187 (pbk.) | ISBN 9781499447194 (library bound) | ISBN 9781499447200 (ebook)
Subjects: LCSH: Egypt--Juvenile literature.
Classification: LCC DT49.B375 2025 | DDC 962--dc23

Manufactured in the United States of America

CPSIA Compliance Information: Batch #CSPK25. For further information contact Rosen Publishing at 1-800-237-9932.

Find us on

Image Credits

All images are courtesy of Shutterstock.com, unless otherwise specified. With thanks to Getty Images, Thinkstock Photo and iStockphoto. Cover – AlexAnton, OAnderson, Sun_Shine, Anna Kosheleva, GoodStudio. 2 – AlexAnton. 4–5 – Andrei Minsk, AlexAnton. 6–7 – givaga, AlexAnton. 8–9 – agsaz, enciktepstudio. 10–11 – oneinchpunch, Pixel-Shot. 12–13 – MalikNalik, ZouZou. 14–15 – dotshock, givaga, Lachlan von Nubia. 16–17 – Pixel-Shot, arapix. 18–19 – Hafizussalam bin Sulaiman, Quisquilia. 20–21 – Alexandree, MaraZe, innakreativ, Pixel-Shot. 22–23 – givaga, tezzstock, John Kasawa, Paulrommer SL.

CONTENTS

Words that look like this can be found in the glossary on page 24.

WHERE IS EGYPT?

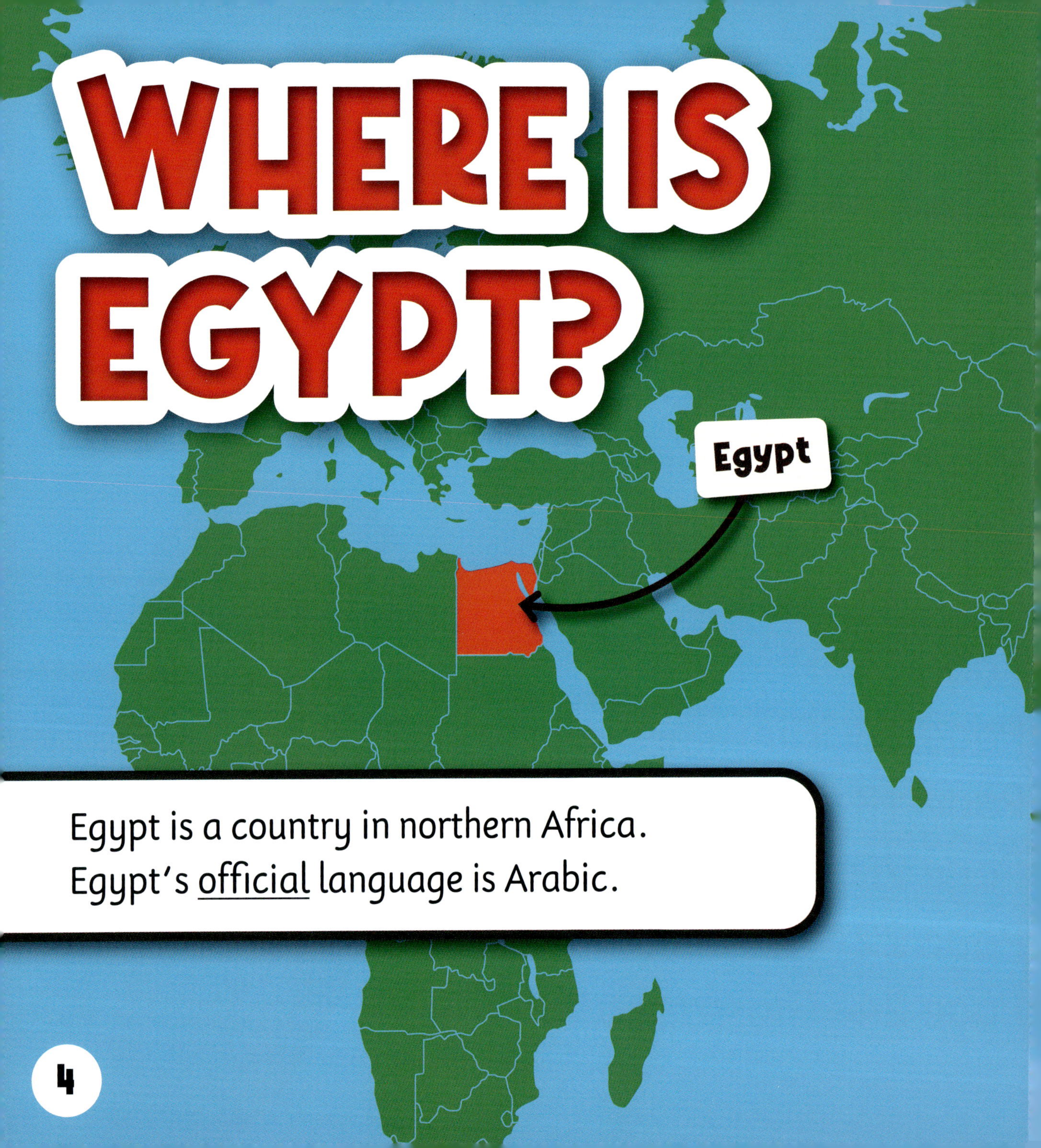

Egypt is a country in northern Africa. Egypt's official language is Arabic.

The capital city of Egypt is called Cairo. Cairo is the biggest city in Egypt.

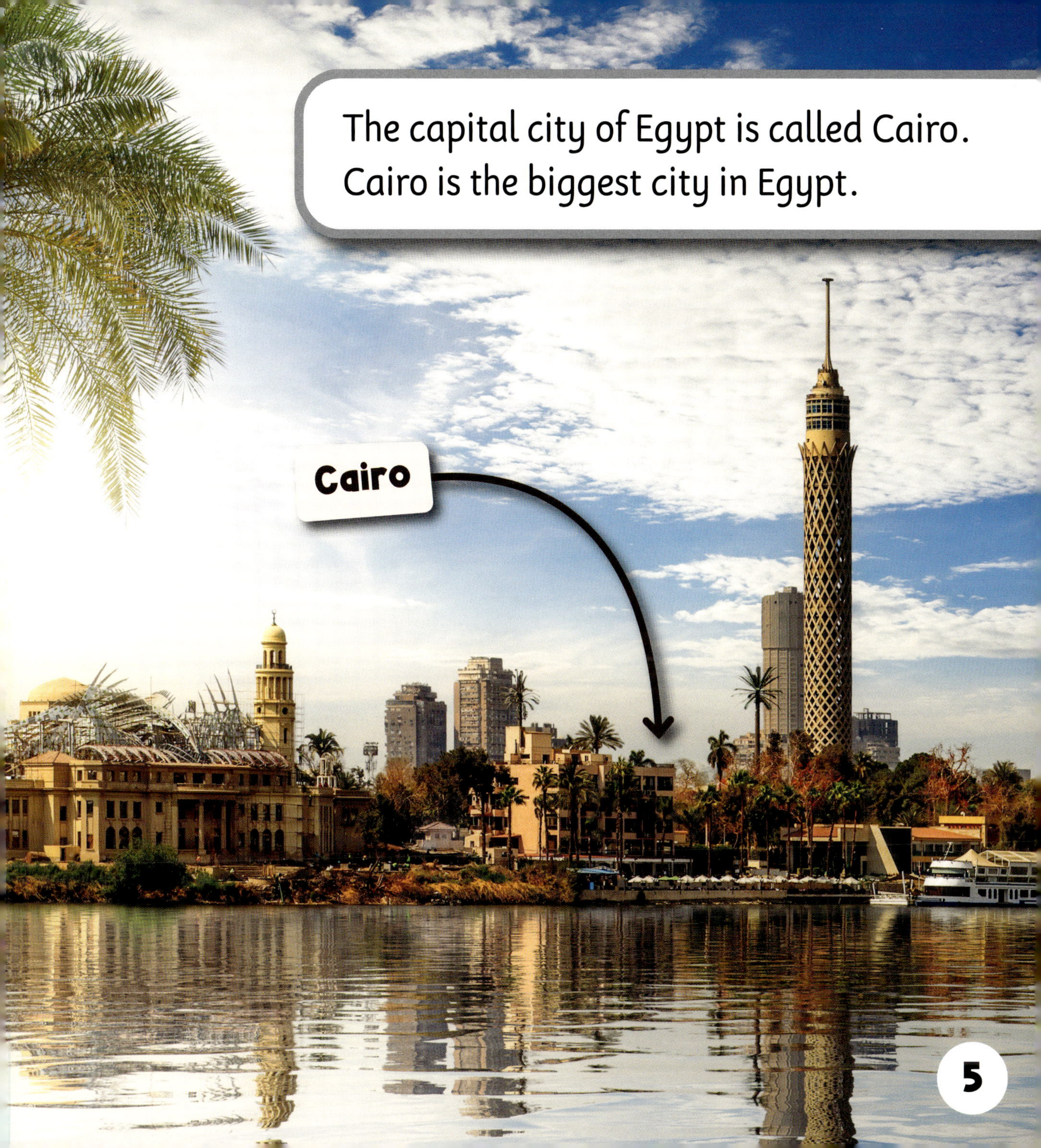

LANDSCAPE AND WEATHER

Most of Egypt is rocky or sandy desert with a hot and dry climate. It has very hot summers and mild winters.

Nearly everyone lives near the Nile River. They use the river for water, food, and transportation.

The Nile is the longest river in the world.

RELIGION

The religion that is most followed in Egypt is Islam. People who follow Islam are called Muslims. Their place of worship is called a mosque.

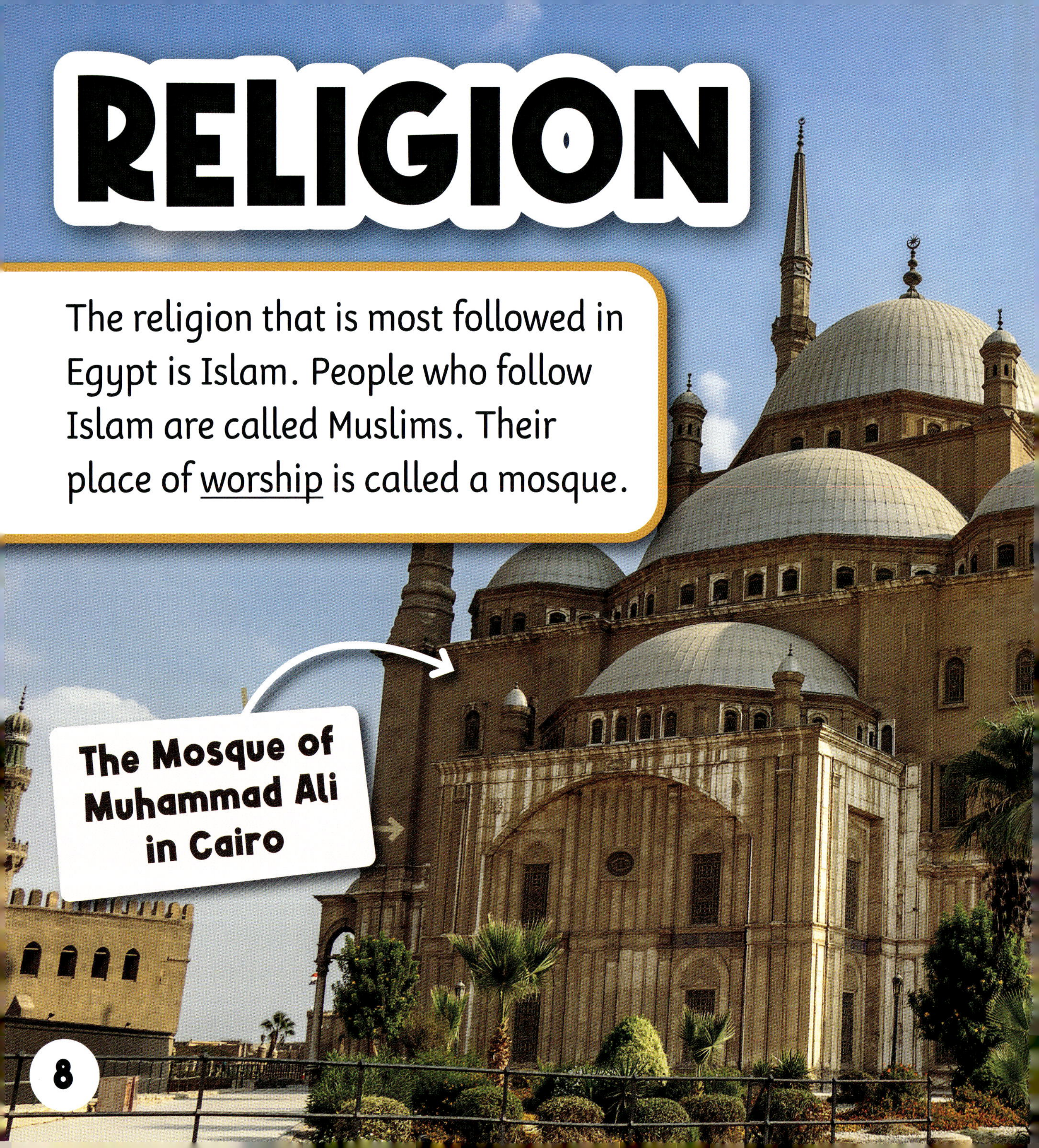

The Mosque of Muhammad Ali in Cairo

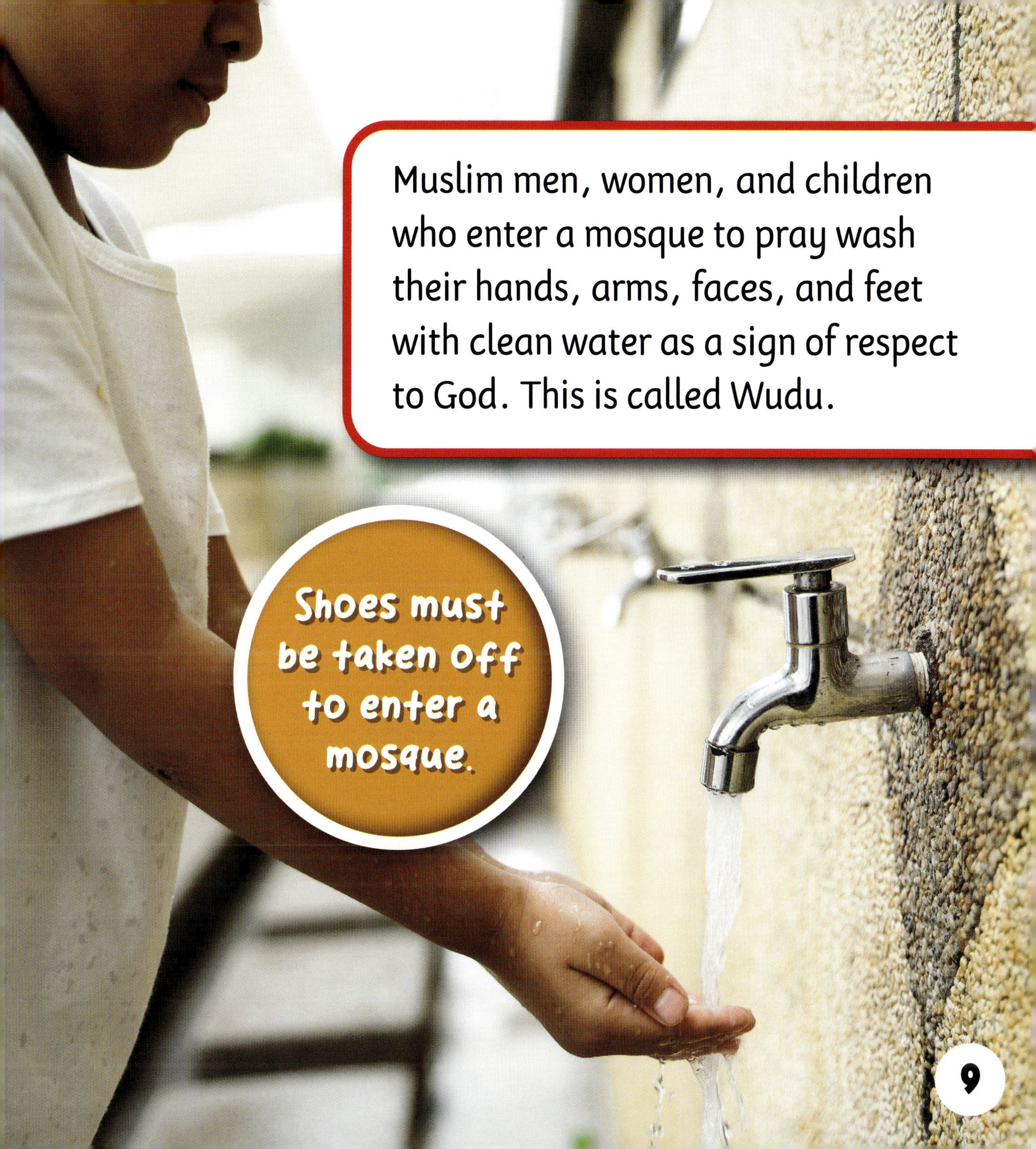

Muslim men, women, and children who enter a mosque to pray wash their hands, arms, faces, and feet with clean water as a sign of respect to God. This is called Wudu.

Shoes must be taken off to enter a mosque.

FAMILIES

Many Egyptian families have more than one generation living in the same home.

Families get together for special occasions such as birthdays and weddings.

SCHOOL

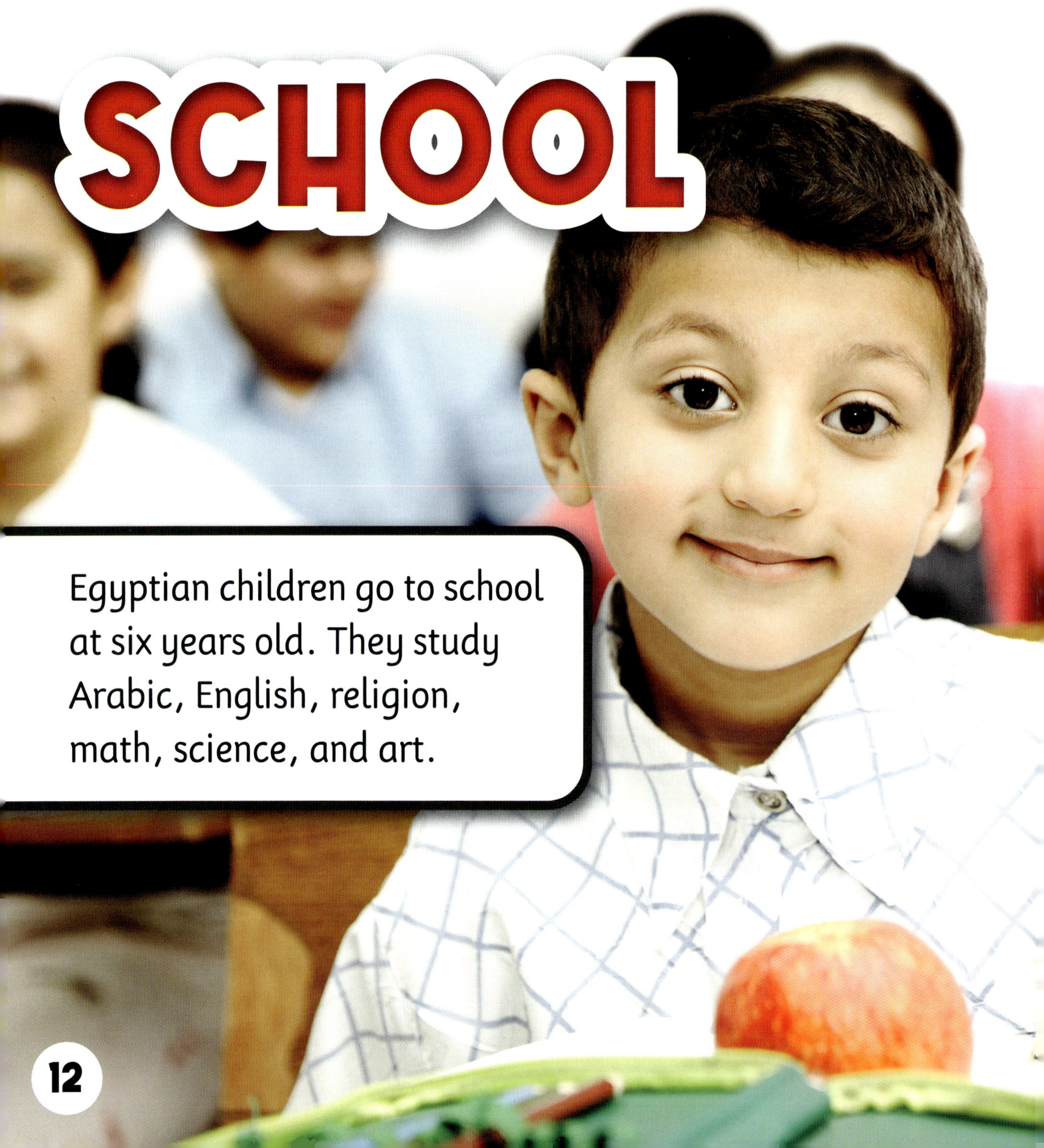

Egyptian children go to school at six years old. They study Arabic, English, religion, math, science, and art.

Children do not go to school on Friday as it is a Muslim holy day. Instead, they may visit the mosque for prayer.

HOME

Egyptian families can be very large and they often live together.

Some families live in mud-brick houses with flat roofs. Others live in modern apartments in the cities.

CLOTHING

Egyptian men often wear loose clothes to keep cool. Some also wear a cloth hat called a taqiyah.

Many Egyptian women wear long dresses and headscarves. This headscarf is called a hijab.

SPORTS

Soccer is the national sport in Egypt. Many children like to play soccer after school with their friends.

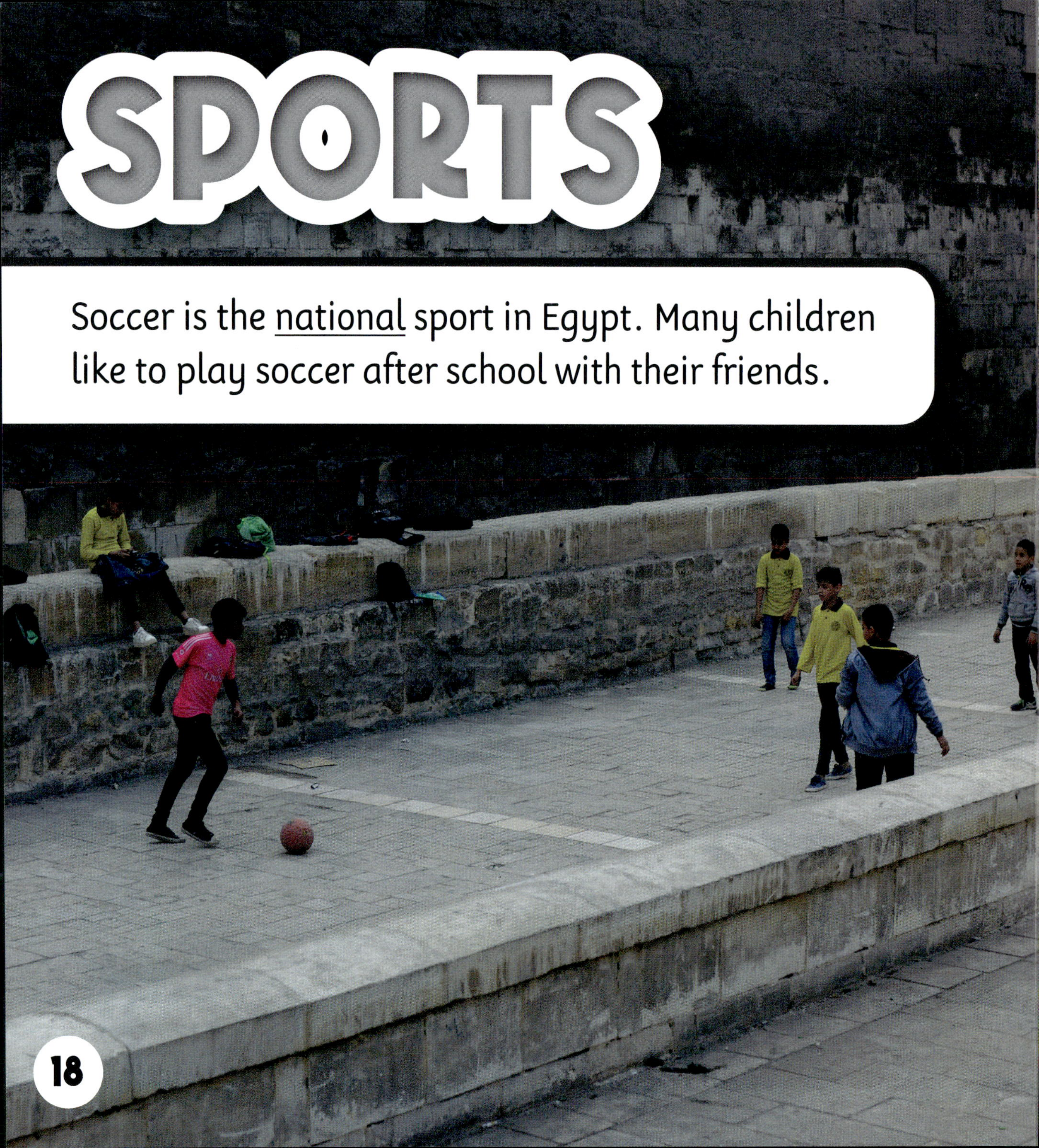

Egyptian children also like to play basketball, handball, and tennis.

FOOD

Egyptians mainly eat wheat bread, rice, and vegetables that are grown in the large fields next to the Nile. They sometimes eat fresh fish from the Nile and the Red Sea.

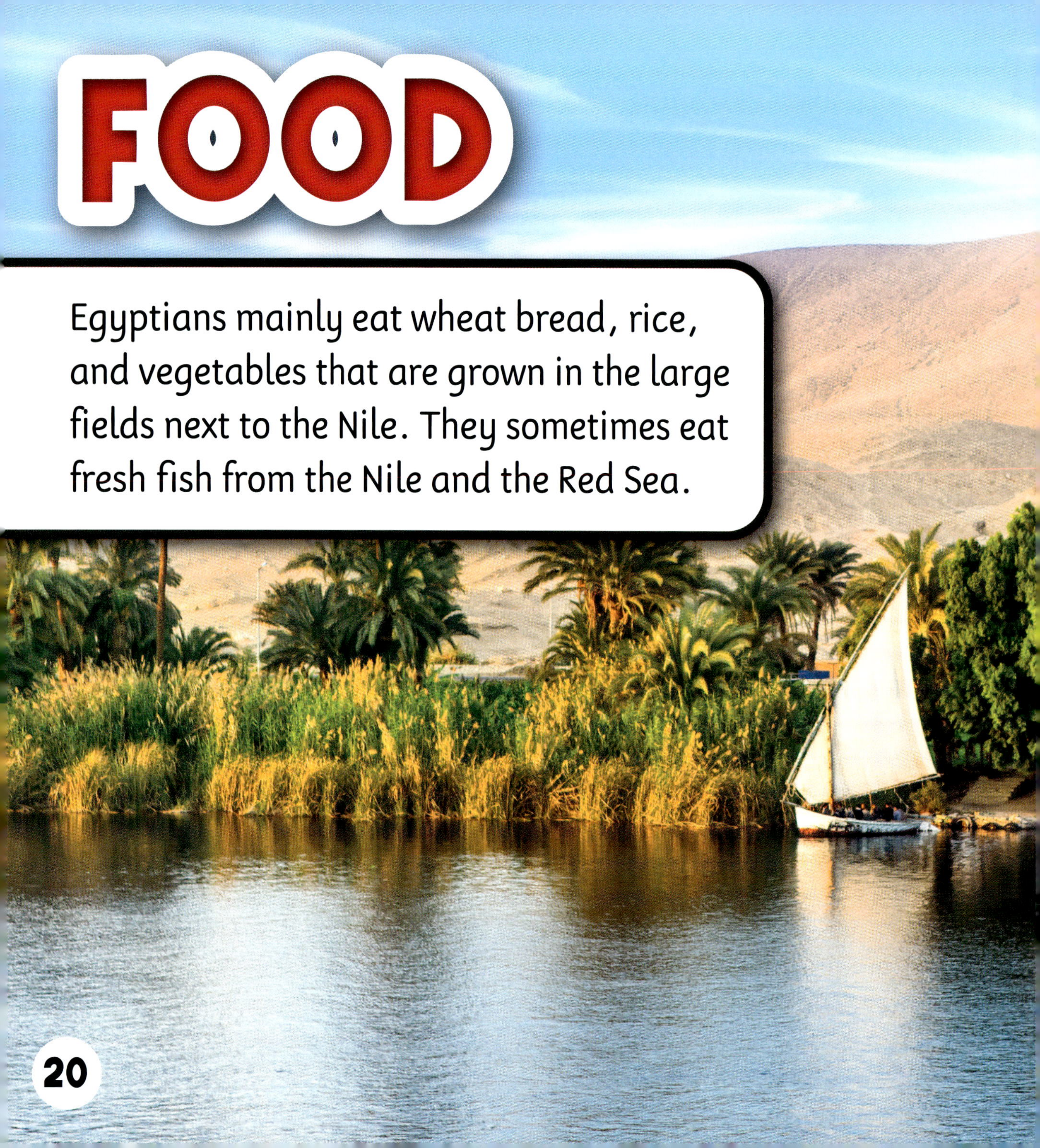

An Egyptian meal often starts with lots of small, healthy dishes, such as falafel and hummus. They can both be made from chickpeas.

FUN FACTS

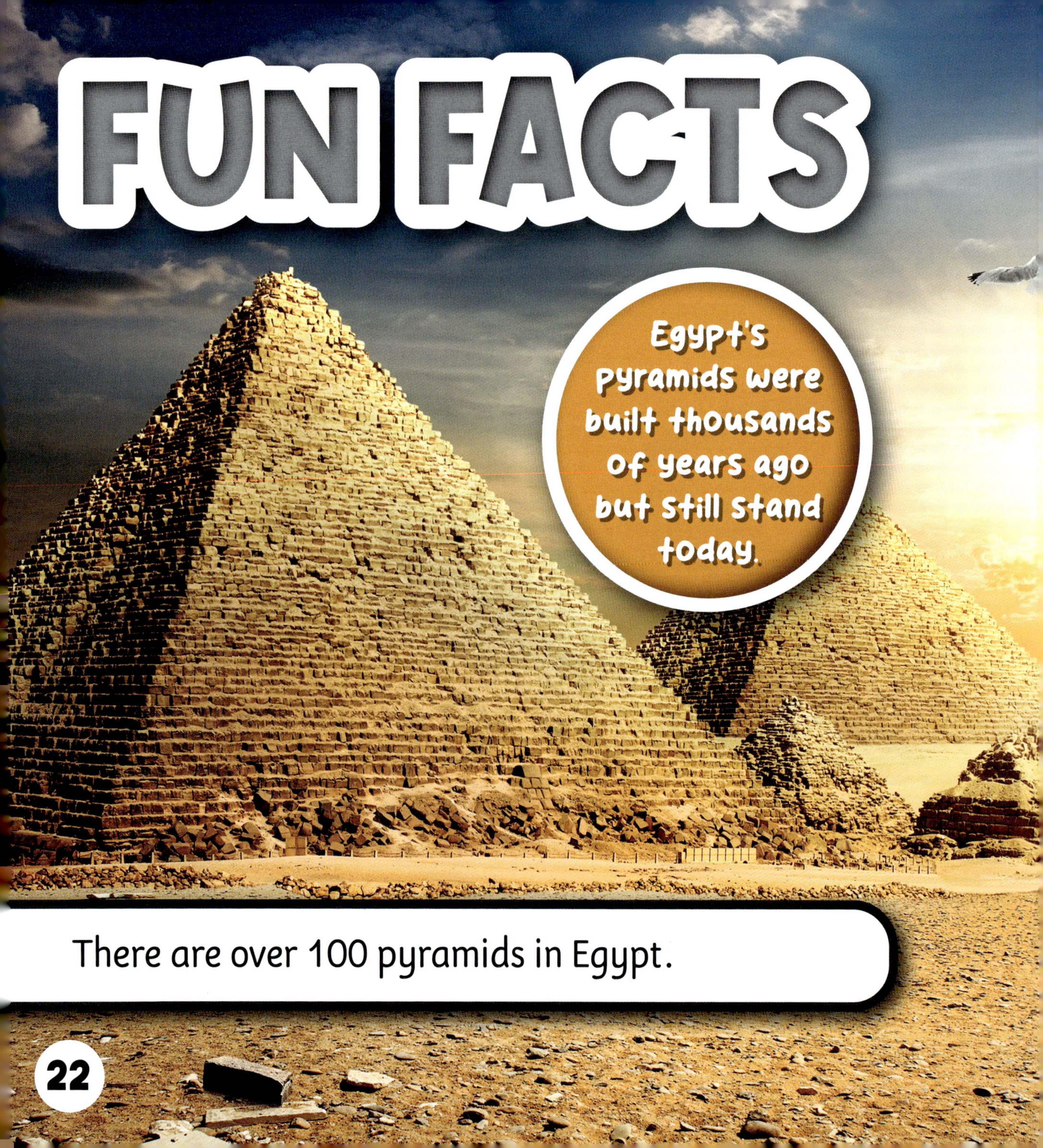

Egypt's pyramids were built thousands of years ago but still stand today.

There are over 100 pyramids in Egypt.

Egypt is home to a large number of animals, including camels, crocodiles, and dung beetles.

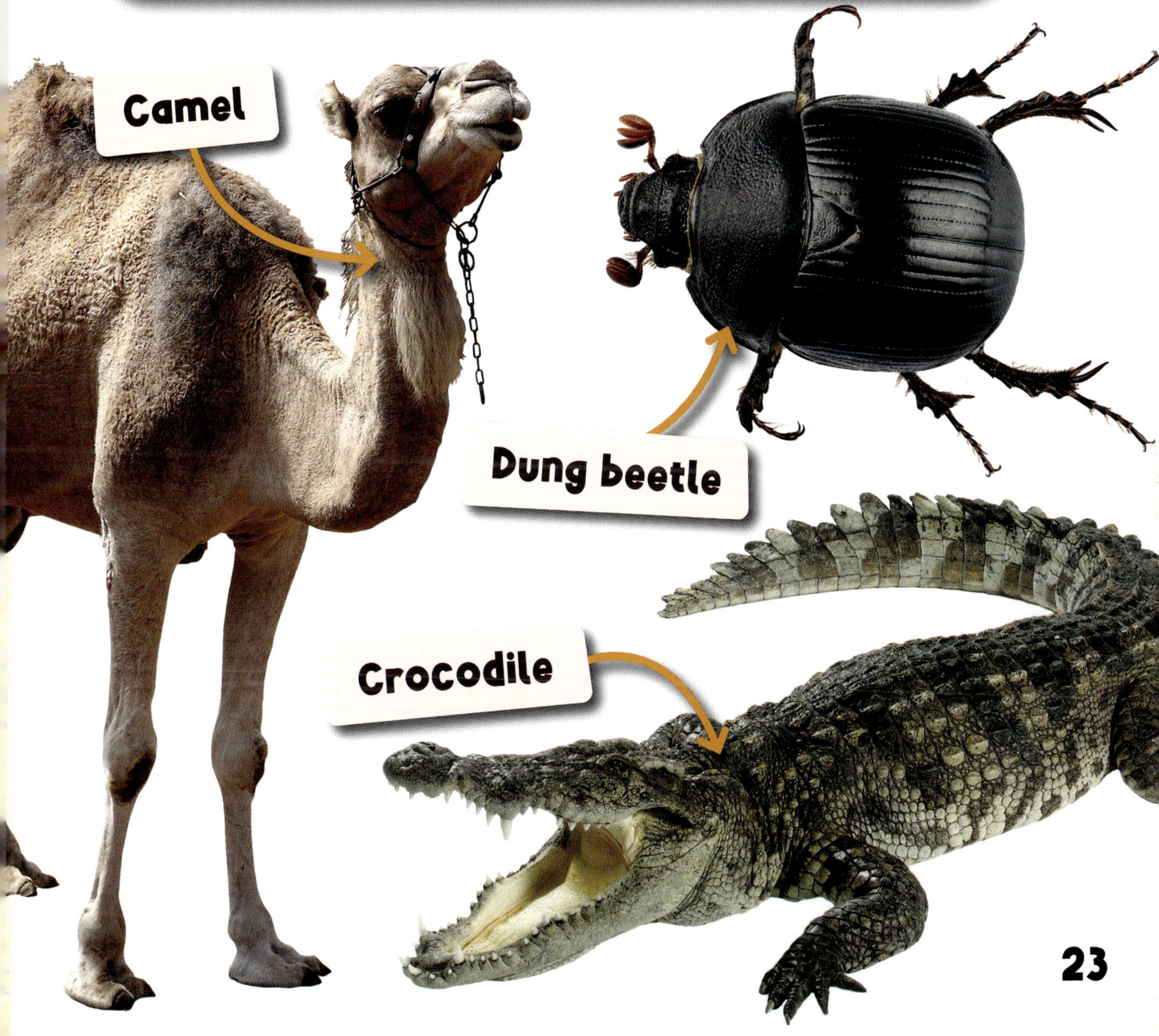

GLOSSARY

climate the weather in a large area

generation a group of people from the same family or society who are roughly the same age

modern something from present or recent times

national having to do with things that are shared by people in a country

occasions special events to celebrate

official having to do with something that is recognized as having power or being important

transportation a way of getting from one place to another

worship a religious act, such as praying

INDEX